# With Love, For You!

From: ..........................................

To: ..........................................

# I Love the way you share

..................................

# With me

It is a curious thought, but it is only when you see people looking ridiculous that you realize just how much you love them.

Agatha Christie

I love you because you make me laugh when you

..........................................

"When you find that one that's right for you, you feel like they were put there for you, you never want to be apart."

Joe Manganiello

# I Love the way you taught me how to

..........................................

"To be fully seen by somebody, then, and be loved anyhow – this is a human offering that can border on miraculous."
			Elizabeth Gilbert

I Love the way you

..............................

In the morning

"Passion makes the world go 'round.
Love just makes it a safer place."

Ice-T

# I love you because you tell me I'm

..............................................

"There is always some madness in love. But there is also always some reason in madness."

Friedrich Nietzsche

# You are special because

..........................................

"Love isn't something natural. Rather it requires discipline, concentration, patience, faith, and the overcoming of narcissism. It isn't a feeling, it is a practice."  Eric Fromm

# I started to have interest in you when

..........................................

I swear I couldn't love you more than I do right now, and yet I know I will tomorrow.

Leo Christopher

# You are more beautful/handso me when

..........................................

"In love there are two things: bodies and words."

Joyce Carol Oates

# I am never going to forget when

..........................................

"There's all kinds of reasons that you fall in love with one person rather than another: Timing is important. Proximity is important. Mystery is important."

Helen Fisher

# One of my dearest memories with you is

..................................................

"I believe in love. I think it just hits you and pulls the rug out from underneath you and, like a baby, demands your attention every minute of the day."

Jodi Picoult

# I love you because you never forget

..........................................

"When you're lucky enough to meet your one person, then life takes a turn for the best. It can't get better than that."

John Krasinski

# I always smile when

..........................................

"You know it's love when all you want is that person to be happy, even if you're not part of their happiness."

Julia Roberts

# As if it was yesterday when

..............................................

"In real love, you want the other person's good. In romantic love, you want the other person."

Margaret Anderson

# Nobody can

..............................................

"To love is to recognize yourself in another."

Eckhart Tolle

# The time spent with you is like

..........................................

"Love has nothing to do with what you are expect to get — only with what you are expecting to give — which is everything."

Katharine Hepburn

# People should have your

..........................................

"In love there are two things: bodies and words."

Joyce Carol Oates

I am never going to forget our trip to

........................................

"Where we love is home – home that our feet may leave, but not our hearts."

Oliver Wendell Holmes Sr.

# I know i can always count on you for

..........................................

"Where there is great love, there are always miracles."

Willa Cather

# I admire your passion for

..........................................

"Love is that condition in which the happiness of another person is essential to your own."

Robert A. Heinlein

I am happy that we neve ever stoop

..........................................

"Have enough courage to trust love one more time and always one more time."

Maya Angelou

# If i had to describe you with only one word it would be

..........................................

"When you realize you want to spend the rest of your life with sombody, you want the rest of your life to start as soon as possible."

Nora Ephron

I wish i were as

..................................

As you

"I'm just a big believer in 'you must love yourself before you can love anybody else' and I think for me that breeds the most inspired relationships."

Scarlett Johansson

# I love that we are so good

........................................

"When you are missing someone, time seems to move slower, and when I'm falling in love with someone, time seems to be moving faster."

Taylor Swift

You know

........................

The best

"Lots of people want to ride with you in the limo, but what you want is someone who will take the bus with you when the limo breaks down."

Oprah Winfrey

I love you because you have the greatest taste in

..........................................

"I love you not only for what you are, but for what I am when I am with you."

Roy Croft

# I love your eyes when you

..........................................

"You found parts of me I didn't know exists and in you I fould a love I no longer believed was real."

Unknown

# You are sexy even when

..............................................

Love does not dominate; it cultivates.

Johann Wolfgang von Goethe

# I love how you always manage to

..........................................

It is a curious thought, but it is only when you see people looking ridiculous that you realize just how much you love them.

Agatha Christie

# You make me feel

..........................................

There is only one happiness in this life, to love and be loved.

George Sand

# You always care about

..........................................

"Love makes your soul crawl out from its hiding place."

Maya Angelou

www.ingramcontent.com/pod-product-compliance
Lightning Source LLC
Chambersburg PA
CBHW072021290426
44109CB00018B/2308